two walking as one

rediscovering your purpose in marriage

HAMP LEE III

(com)mission PUBLISHING

MONTGOMERY, ALABAMA

Copyright © 2019 by Hamp Lee III

All rights reserved.

No part of this publication may be reproduced, distributed or transmitted in any form or by any means, including photocopying, recording, or other electronic or mechanical methods, without the prior written permission of the publisher, except in the case of brief quotations embodied in critical reviews and certain other non-commercial uses permitted by copyright law. For permission requests, write the publisher at info@commissionpubs.com.

Recommendations within *Two Walking As One: Rediscovering Your Purpose in Marriage* are for informational and educational purposes only. Please consult with the appropriate (and respective) professionals, agencies, or groups before acting on the information in this book.

Scripture quotations taken from the Amplified® Bible (AMP),
Copyright © 2015 by The Lockman Foundation Used by permission.

Scripture quotations marked KJV are from the King James Version of the Bible, public domain.

Scripture quotations marked (WEB) are taken from the WORLD ENGLISH BIBLE, public domain.

Two Walking As One: Rediscovering Your Purpose in Marriage/
Hamp Lee III.—1st ed.

Library of Congress Control Number: 2019912833
ISBN: 978-1-940042-64-0

contents

INTRODUCTION	5
1. APPLYING AMOS	9
2. WALKING WORTHY (PART I)	13
3. WALKING WORTHY (PART I)	15
4. LEARNING ABOUT THE "ONE"	17
5. SUNDAY STROLL	29
6. HUSBAND AND WIFE ROLES	31
7. MARRIAGE MISSION STATEMENT	35
8. A HOUSE DIVIDED	41
9. DAILY WALKS	45
10. SUNDAY STROLL	49
CONCLUSION	51
ENDNOTES	53

introduction

Many people marry for the pursuit of happiness, peace, and love. They want to spend the rest of their lives in joyful bliss. And though there are many dreams of a beautiful, successful, and peaceful marriage, many people don't know how to make it a reality in their lives for one week, let alone a lifetime.

Some might find that having a beautiful, successful, and peaceful marriage is a lot different when two people come together from different backgrounds and experiences. Frustration sets in. Stress is magnified. Dreams are shattered. You try as hard as you can to find your way back to your expectations and dreams only to have them thrown back in your face. Unable to change the direction of your marriage or the heart of the person you committed to love, you settle for far less than your ideal.

Some of the things you do to survive the pain and heartbreak in your marriage could be considered healthy, and others are destructive to yourself and your marriage. You're trying to make it to "forever," wearing a mask to cover the pain you have inside. Where you thought you would walk joyfully with your partner, you find your journey is filled with everything but joy. Joy, as well as peace, seem unfathomable against the years of hurt and pain calloused around your minds and hearts.

Sometimes couples lose sight of why they married. Maybe they couldn't get past their past. There was no direction on how to walk together in holy matrimony. Some give up because they didn't have the answers and were tired of trying again and again. They were afraid of being hurt once more. But not all troubled marriages have to remain in this state or end in divorce…

You can walk with your spouse.

You can travel along roads of happiness, joy, and peace in the Holy Spirit.

You can make it to your destination.

I wrote *Two Walking As One: Rediscovering Your Purpose in Marriage* to help struggling marriages. Many couples are silently hurting and suffering through feelings of loneliness, hopelessness, and discouragement. They cover their scars and pains from a marriage that became everything they never hoped for. So Lord willing, this study guide can provide couples with a few simple tools, resources, and information to establish a loving, mutually-edifying union before God.

Prayerfully, you'll be able to read this study guide with your spouse. Because it's not a long read, it's meant to start a discussion, and Lord willing, a habit that can help you build upon the foundation of Jesus Christ as walk together as one (1 Corinthians 3:11).

Designed as a 15-30 minute daily study, make it a priority to study together each day, whether at the beginning of the day or before you go to bed. If possible, study at the same time each day for consistency. My personal recommendation is to study in the morning.

When you study, you may not get through an entire chapter in 15-30 minutes. Don't worry about trying to complete a chapter a day. Bookmark where you stop and start again at your next study time. The goal here is to build a consistent habit of prayer, worship, and study together.

When starting the study, begin with prayer, and even a song of worship if you like; something you both can share. Have a notebook or note-taking application available to write your responses, thoughts, or messages from the lessons.

The first section in this study guide addresses your personal walk with the Lord and the second, walking together with your spouse. There are also two Sunday Stroll messages. These messages are meant for deeper reflection from the previous section.

I want to thank you for using this study guide to help you learn how you can walk together with your spouse. I pray your lives together will be forever changed because of the message God shares in these pages.

applying Amos

Can two walk together, except they be agreed?
Amos 3:3 KJV

When many people quote Amos 3:3, they often use it in the context of marital relationships. But when Amos spoke this verse to the people of Israel, they were receiving a word spoken against them from the Lord for their continuous sin (Amos 2:6-4:5). From Amos 3:3-6, the Lord was describing several things that would not be able to happen. This was in reference to what the Lord was about to do as He revealed it through the prophets.

From the judgment pronounced against Israel, one of the lessons you can draw from their lives is to be faithful to the Lord, living in obedience and holiness before Him. See, the most important relationship in your life should be with God. Though some would consider their marriage to be their most important relationship, its purposes lie in procreation, supporting one another in his or her God-given call and mission, and reflecting the marital relationship between Christ and His bride, the church, on earth (Ephesians 5:22-33).

Another purpose husbands and wives should have is wanting one another to hear Jesus say, "well done thy good and faithful servant" (Matthew 25:21). But first, I believe it's important to ensure you're walking in agreement with the Lord by living righteously before Him:

As you abide in the Lord, He will show you the path of life that allows you to glorify Him and experience man's highest aim: the fullness of joy.

Let's take a moment to break down three important messages from the quote above.

1. Abide in the Lord. When addressing His disciples before His betrayal, Jesus spoke about them abiding in three things: abiding in Him (John 15:1-5; Hebrews 12:11), His word (John 15:7), and His love by obeying His commandments (John 15:9-11). The word 'abide' is translated as to stay, continue, dwell, endure, be present, remain, stand, and tarry. This 'abiding' is a commitment to the Lord, in and through your life circumstances. There will be seasons where it seems easy to abide in Jesus and others, you'll need to persevere through, counting your various temptations as a joy (James 1:2-4).

2. Show us the path of life (Psalm 16:11). As you abide in Jesus, He'll show you the path that leads you into His presence forever. As the writer describes in Hebrews 11:32-40, there will be some who experience great triumphs and others, great tragedy. But as a couple, you both must live faithfully through the life God assigns to you to reflect His glory (John 9:2-3; 1 Peter 4:12-15). You'll each have an individual purpose, but in coming together as one in marriage, you'll also have a corporate purpose the Lord give the husband (Genesis 2:15-18).

3. Bear fruit. Your highest aim in this life will be to experience the fullness of joy in God's presence in eternity (Psalm 16:11). His highest aim for you is to bring Him glory by bearing fruit as He prepares you to be with Him forever (Isaiah 43:7; Matthew 5:14-16, 7:15-20). As you abide in Jesus, He'll prune you so you can bear more fruit (John15:2). As you bear more fruit, you and your spouse will walk together along the path of life with love and support (Psalm 119:105).

walking worthy (part 1)

I therefore, the prisoner in the Lord, beg you to walk worthily of the calling with which you were called, with all lowliness and humility, with patience, bearing with one another in love
Ephesians 4:1-2 WEB

There are many callings and positions you'll assume in your life. Husband. Wife. Mother. Father. Friend. Volunteer. Supervisor. Ephesians 4 shows that the highest calling you can ever assume is that of a believer in Christ. And Ephesians 4:1-2 outlines four attributes for walking worthy of the calling you have been called.

Reviewing Ephesians 4:1-2, in what four ways can you walk worthy of the calling you have been called?

Using a bible or standard dictionary, define each of these four attributes. Review 1 Corinthians 13:1-8 as well.

Read Ephesians 4:1-2 in the Amplified Bible. What expanded attributes can you incorporate in your life to walk worthy of the calling you have been called as a believer in Christ? Include each attribute with the four listed above.

So I, the prisoner for the Lord, appeal to you to live a life worthy of the calling to which you have been called [that is, to live a life that exhibits godly character, moral courage, personal integrity, and mature behavior--a life that expresses gratitude to God for your salvation], with all humility [forsaking self-righteousness], and gentleness [maintaining self-control], with patience, bearing with one another in [unselfish] love.
Ephesians 4:1-2 AMP

walking worthy (part II)

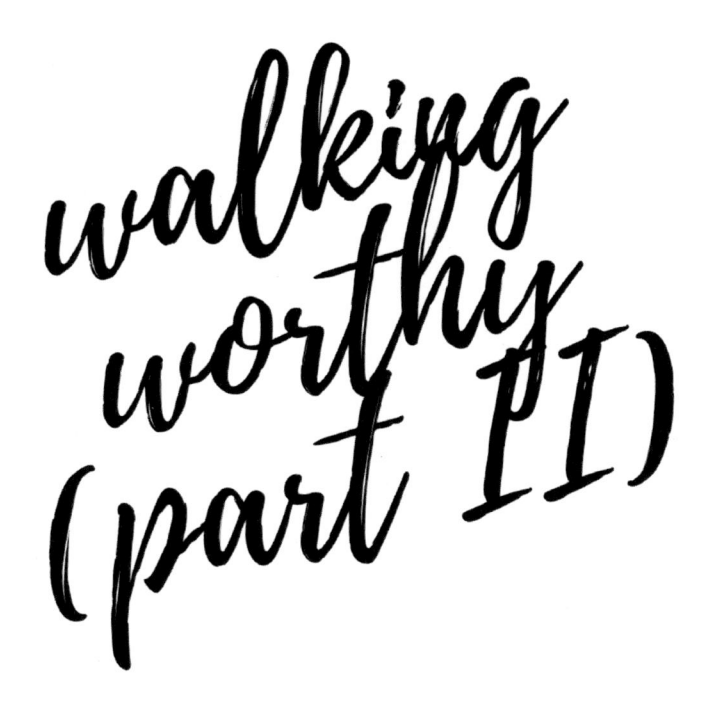

Read Ephesians 4:17-32.

List each of the ways from Ephesians 4:17-32 you can walk worthy of the calling you have been called as a believer in Jesus.

Which attribute from Ephesians 4:17-32 has been the most challenging (and helpful) for you?

Meditate on your list throughout the week and ask the Lord to help you incorporate each one into your life.

learning about the "one"

Two becoming one is a process of learning how each person lives individually to walk in a loving, mutually-edifying relationship.

As you walk worthy of your calling as a believer of Jesus Christ, you're also walking with your spouse. Becoming one in marriage is two separate people coming together with different upbringings and experiences. And as you bring these differences together, you might spend a lifetime learning about one another. But knowing the differences you have is more than learning husbands like to leave the toilet seat up and wives like collecting cat figurines. It's learning about one another and discovering how to navigate your union in a loving and mutually-edifying manner.

Therefore shall a man leave his father and his mother, and shall cleave unto his wife: and they shall be one flesh.
Genesis 2:24 KJV

One of the biblical descriptions for the word 'one' in Genesis 2:24 is being alike. Being alike doesn't mean you wear the same clothes. It means you share similar thoughts and purposes. This is why learning about one another is so important. To walk together purposefully, you must share the same destination in Christ, actively support your individual, marital, and spiritual goals, and learn about any benefits or challenges that might affect your marriage or walk with Christ.

Likewise, ye husbands, dwell with them according to knowledge, giving honour unto the wife, as unto the weaker vessel, and as being heirs together of the grace of life; that your prayers be not hindered.
1 Peter 3:7 KJV

As with the husband, I believe the wife should also dwell with her husband according to knowledge. In 1 Peter 3:7, two words stand out: dwell and knowledge.

The biblical definition of 'dwell' in 1 Peter 3:7 means to reside together as a family. But residing together as a family is a lot different from living in a house together. Husbands and wives can be in the same house but not know one another or share any love, mutually-edifying behaviors, or specific actions toward fulfilling God's purpose in their lives.

'Knowing' is acquiring information about another person. And as a couple, it'll be important to learn as much as you can: good, bad, and everything in-between.

In the coming days, spend time learning about one another. The knowledge you gain, or information you discuss is not about whether you like vanilla ice cream or watching a specific movie. These conversations should be specifically purposed to learn about one another in such a way that you can live together in a loving and mutually-edifying manner. Your discussions don't have to be overly formal, but they should be consistent and deliberate.

Will there be differences? Yes.

Will you need to work out how to best live together with those differences? Yes.

Will you need to speak to one another in a loving, non-combative manner (Ephesians 4:29)? Yes.

Will you need to work toward compromises, partnership, understanding one another, and active listening? Yes.

When discussing the following topics, please ensure you both are open, honest, and patient. Your desire should be to hear what the other person is saying, understand what they are saying, and identify his or her perspective.

Some of the questions might be considered extremely sensitive. Though sensitive, they might reveal hidden pains and emotions that drive your decisions today and keep you captive to your past. The purpose of these questions isn't to unearth old wounds but to address areas of your life that may impact your marriage today. Please seek professional counseling and support resources where necessary.

Discussion Questions

Childhood

1. Describe your family upbringing and dynamic.

2. What significant events from your childhood impact your life as an adult today?

3. Were one or both of your parents dependent on alcohol, drugs, or some other substance? If so, describe your feelings and how your parent(s)' actions affected you.

4. Was there a lot of yelling, name-calling, or domestic abuse in your household growing up? If so, please describe how it impacted you as a child, and now as an adult.

5. Describe "family time" in your home?

6. Who were the people you looked up to growing up? Describe why you looked up to them.

7. Were you sexually assaulted or raped as a child? If so, have you sought help? If those heinous acts negatively impacted your life decisions and marriage today, please describe how.

8. Were you physically or verbally abused as a child? If so, have you sought help? If those instances of abuse negatively impacted your life decisions and marriage today, please describe how.

Communication

1. Has your parents' communication style impacted how you communicate with your spouse? If so, please explain.

2. Of the four communication styles, which do you most associate with:[1]

Aggressive. Speaks in a loud and demanding voice, maintains intense eye contact and dominates or controls others by blaming, intimidating, criticizing, threatening, or attacking them.

Assertive. Opens communication link while not being overbearing; expresses their own needs, desires, ideas, and feelings, while also considering the needs of others.

Passive-Aggressive. Appears passive on the surface, but within he or she may feel powerless or stuck, building up a resentment that leads to seething or acting out in subtle, indirect, or secret ways.

Passive. Often acts indifferently, yielding to others; fails to express their feelings or needs.

3. Do you spend time each day and week talking to your spouse about the events of your day?

4. Do you feel comfortable talking to your spouse about your challenges, stresses, times of depression, or other negative emotions or experiences? Please explain.

5. What is your spouse's communication style?

Conflict Resolution

1. How did your parents resolve their conflicts? Is this how you resolve your conflicts now? If it is, please explain how this is positive or negative for your marriage.

2. Of the five methods for resolving conflicts, which do you most associate with:[2]

Accommodating. Sacrifices one's own goals for the sake of the other person.

Avoiding. Behaviors that either ignore or refuse to engage in the conflict.

Compromising. Negotiating to "split the difference" between two positions.

Collaborating. Cooperatively working together until a mutually-agreeable solution is found.

Competing. Maximizes reaching one's own goals or getting the problem solved at the cost of the other person's intentions or feelings.

3. How often do you incorporate prayer and the bible into conflict resolution? Do you believe this will help you and your spouse resolve more conflicts? Why or why not?

Extended Family Life

1. Does your father, mother, brother, sister, etc. (extended family) have a considerable influence over your decision making?

2. How "involved" is your extended family in your marriage?

3. Discuss your desires for the family-in-law's involvement in your marriage?

Family

1. Do you have children from a previous relationship? If so, what are the parental dynamic and the expectation/role of your spouse as the step-parent?

2. Do you desire to have children together? If so, how many?

3. What are your views on child-rearing (discipline)?

4. How has your childhood upbringing affected how you raise (or would like to raise) your children?

5. Do you have any established family traditions (e.g., weekly or seasonal)? If so, please describe.

6. Do you plan date nights or go on family trips and vacations? If so, please explain.

Financial Responsibilities

1. Are you bringing any debt into the marriage? If so, please discuss all obligations.

2. What are your views on money and financial responsibility?

3. Would you say you're a big spender, penny pincher, or like to buy a lot of little "things?"

4. Will you have a one- or two-person income in your household? Please explain.

5. Do you have a workable budget?

6. What are your financial goals? Do you both share the same goals? Please explain.

7. Will your banking accounts be joint or separate? Why?

Goals and Purposes

1. Do you know what God's purpose is for your life? If so, please explain.

2. Do you know what God's purpose is for your spouse? If so, please explain.

3. What are your personal goals? Career goals? Family goals?

4. What legacy would you like to leave your spouse, children, and the world?

5. Do you know your spouse's life goals and purposes?

6. Do you and your spouse have shared goals and purposes? If so, what are they?

Household Responsibilities

1. How are household responsibilities divided (e.g., paying bills, cleaning, cooking)?

2. Is there an expectation to share responsibilities? Why or why not?

Religious Beliefs

1. Do you share the same religious beliefs as your spouse? Please explain.

2. How often do you and your spouse pray or read the bible together?

3. How often does your family pray or read the bible together?

sunday stroll

What has been the most impactful message(s) or lesson(s) from this first section?

Describe what it means to abide in Jesus and His word and love.

Reviewing the two chapters on walking worthy, make a personal commitment to incorporate each attribute in your life, and pray for your spouse to do the same.

Did you learn things about your spouse that you didn't know before? If so, please explain.

Summarize your experiences in learning about one another.

husband and wife roles

The first section was spent learning about yourself and a little about your spouse. I hope you were able to learn some great things about yourself and your relationship with Christ, as well as your spouse and his or her relationship with Christ.

Knowing more about your spouse is important so you can understand how to walk together. The decisions you make and the perspectives you hold are based on past decisions and experiences, and these often impact the direction you and your spouse walk in. Sadly for some couples, they spend years feeling as if they are walking alone or in different directions rather than together. But learning about yourself and your spouse is a significant first step in your lifelong endeavor.

So in this section, let's focus on how you and your spouse can walk together. I want to start with the biblical roles assigned to both husbands and wives.

Throughout the cultures of the world, you might find many different norms concerning the roles of a husband and wife. But as a Christian, you both want to know God's standard.

In scripture, the biblical order for the husband and wife is that the husband is above the wife as Christ is above the husband (1 Corinthians 11:3; Ephesians 5:23). This doesn't mean the husband lords over his wife or treats her in a degrading manner. He is to love her as Christ loves the church (Ephesians 5:25). In mutual respect, the wife is to love and submit to her husband, providing a union of oneness, love, and purpose as they walk together before the Father.

Please review the following scriptures for both the husband and wife. Before moving to the next chapter, please take a moment to summarize your views on the biblical roles of husbands and wives. Using these scriptures, discuss ways you both can walk together in matrimony.

Husband

Genesis 2:23-24; Proverbs 5:15-19, 13:22, 18:22, 31:10-12; Ecclesiastes 9:9; 1 Corinthians 7:3-5, 14-16; Ephesians 5:25-33; Colossians 3:19; 1 Timothy 5:8

Wife

Proverbs 12:4, 14:1, 19:13-14, 21:9, 25:24, 31:10-31; Ephesians 5:22-23; Colossians 3:18; 1 Peter 3:1-7

marriage mission statement

Sadly, many marriages move aimlessly through life without direction or purpose. Husbands and wives go through the same redundant actions each week to survive to the next week. They try to make it through the day's challenges without arguing or experiencing any significant incidents? *But can that be considered as walking together?*

Would you find large organizations or colleges running aimlessly, trying to make it to the next week or year without purpose, direction, or incidents? No. They have mission statements that purposefully center their efforts in a particular area, field, and direction. And as they know the "why" of their existence, I believe your marriage shouldn't be any different.

As you come together in marriage, you both have separate purposes God gives you in addition to the purpose God gives the husband. So to help focus your marriage in a specific direction and purpose, I suggest establishing a marriage mission statement.

A marriage mission statement is a simple, concise statement that identifies the purpose of your marriage. It's your aim and focus. It says, "this is our goal," and the two of you work toward that goal each day.

In building a marriage mission statement, there are four key points I would like you to consider.

*1. Is the marriage mission statement **mutual**?* Having a mutual marriage mission statement means both of you have a shared "stake" in its creation. It's not enough for one of you to come up with the statement, and other says "approved." This is a process where both of you work to establish a marriage mission statement you both agree on, one you both have invested in.

*2. Is the marriage mission statement **moveable**?* When you read your marriage mission statement, does it encourage you to walk together in a specific and deliberate direction toward your goals?

*3. Is the marriage mission statement **measurable**?* When you review your marriage mission statement, you both should be able to quickly determine whether you're "hitting the goal" of your mission statement.

*4. Is the marriage mission statement **memorable**?* Do you have a long quotation that you can barely memorize or repeat without reading it? Maybe this isn't the right mission statement for your marriage.

Consider the following marriage mission statement:

God first…forever and always.

Let's say both the husband and wife developed this mission statement.

This marriage mission statement is **moveable** because it places the couple on the path of intentionally inviting God into their decisions, thoughts, and actions…first.

This marriage mission statement is **measurable** because with one question, you can discover whether a decision, thought, or action considers God first above anything else.

This marriage mission statement is **memorable** because it's concise, five words.

Now it's your turn.

Take a few moments to consider how you can create a mutual, moveable, measurable, and memorable marriage mission statement. Your marriage mission statement doesn't have to be five words, but I suggest it's not 200 words either. Focus your marriage mission statement on something simple that connects you both to your life purposes in Christ.

1. Pray.

2. Talk about your goals, purposes, and destination.

3. Outline key attributes you would like to emulate toward one another and before God.

4. As you consider your destination through Christ, decide on key scriptures or descriptions you would like to represent your marriage.

5. Summarize your scriptures and descriptions. Develop one to several different marriage mission statement to choose from.

6. Pray.

7. Adjust your statements as the Lord leads and select your marriage mission statement.

8. Create a poster or sign with your marriage mission statement to prominently display in your home or office.

a house divided

Knowing their thoughts Jesus said to them, "Any kingdom that is divided against itself is being laid waste; and no city or house divided against itself will [continue to] stand."
Matthew 12:25 AMP

Replying to the Pharisees who said Jesus was getting His power to cast out demons from Satan, Jesus said that a house divided against itself cannot stand. A house divided is not unified on a shared mission that leads toward a successful outcome. Some want to do one thing, and others want to do another. Resources, time, and unnecessary efforts are expended and wasted because those in the house cannot agree on a common purpose or direction. The house cannot stand.

As you're working to walk together with your spouse, there might be areas or subjects you're currently divided on. You might find yourself feeling defeated, stressed, and hopeless where you give up on the possibility of ever being fulfilled in your marriage. Though you might seem happy on the outside, it's only a mask you use to cover the pain on the inside. This is a far cry from the ideal you had for yourself and your marriage.

And if you're feeling like this in any way, please seek help. Reach out to trusted friends and counselors to help you find healthy and spiritual ways to become mentally, physically, emotionally, and spiritually resilient.

Sometimes the division in a marriage can be resolved with a simple conversation, and other times, a neutral third-party is needed. Please be prayerful about the condition of your heart and mental, physical, emotional, and spiritual state. You want to ensure any heartbreak doesn't become a hard-heart, and pride doesn't lead you to destruction (Proverbs 16:18).

1. If you're able to speak with your spouse peacefully, please consider discussing the issues you believe has brought division between you. Pray about the most convenient time to talk and consider their demeanor and wellness also (Galatians 6:1-2).

2. Keep your focus on the restoration of your marriage and not wanting to "win" or argue for the sake of arguing. You want to be able to honor God in your conduct to restore your marriage and one another before Him.

3. If you feel you can't speak to your spouse peacefully, pray about a time you can ask if he or she is willing to talk with a counselor or trusted, neutral third-party. Don't force your spouse to speak to anyone. You want your spouse to participate voluntarily. If you speak with one another without a mediator, ensure you have the time to unpack the issues on your hearts. Such discussions shouldn't be rushed.

4. Pray before you meet and before you speak.

5. Listen more than you speak. Create a safe environment for your spouse to speak without feeling intimidated or resistant. Use the opportunity to understand what's on your spouse's heart. Even if you might not agree with what's being said, respect their position and perspective of how they see things occurring. Regardless of what you might think, this is their perspective.

6. Thank your spouse for sharing his or her heart and concerns with you. For some spouses, this is a

considerable undertaking to share their concerns due to their upbringing or events in the marriage.

7. Pray about what each of you shared. As Jesus is in the midst of you (Matthew 18:20), ask for His help to resolve your differences and heal your hearts (where needed). Pray for wisdom on establishing a plan for unity.

8. Using your marriage mission statement and relevant scriptures, discuss ways to address any division in your marriage. Ensure there are open lines of communication and mutual agreement.

9. Pray for the recommendations you created.

10. Execute and assess periodically.

daily walks

Make every effort to keep the oneness of the Spirit in the bond of peace [each individual working together to make the whole successful].
Ephesians 5:3 AMP

When Paul wrote this message, he was speaking to the church in Ephesus. Within a context of marriage, I would like to use this message to encourage you and your spouse to make every effort to keep the oneness of the Spirit in the bond of peace.

With the daily troubles that come into our lives (Matthew 6:34), there will be many things that can impact and affect your ability or desire to walk together. And as such, you and your spouse should individually work together to make the whole successful. You both must share in the responsibility of the success of your marriage, not just one of you. This work is deliberate and cooperative to ensure your "oneness" remains intact and you don't become two individuals living in a house as roommates.

The first (and only) "effort" I'll discuss in this chapter is encouraging praying and reading and studying the bible together. As there are 1,440 minutes in a day, I'd like you and your spouse to commit to using 15-30 minutes of each day to pray and read/study. If you think about it, that's only 1 % or 2% of your entire day.

Prayer

As your spouse is your closest neighbor (Matthew 22:39), you can touch and agree each day. For some, it's as simple as throwing your arm across the bed.

But in this setting, I would like to encourage you both to pray together at least 1-2 times each day. For many, this would be in the morning before starting the day or departing for work and in the evening before going to bed. Your prayer doesn't have to be long. It's an opportunity for the two of you to come together to seek the Lord as you walk toward your individual and marital purposes.

There's nothing wrong with praying more times throughout the day via phone or text. You don't have to pray long prayers — just quick moments to touch and agree.

I would also encourage you both to spend one time during the weekend or "slower" time in the week for intercessory prayer together. This can be something as simple as playing praise and worship music as you pray for yourselves, friends, family members, etc.

Bible Reading and Study

In reading or studying the bible, you don't have to establish any formal or in-depth study. This is just an opportunity for both of you to come together. And if you or your spouse aren't comfortable leading or teaching a lesson, you can select a devotional to read together. There are many devotionals you can purchase at a bookstore or online, but YouVersion provides numerous bible reading plans that last anywhere from a few days to one year. (This is not a paid advertisement.)

YouVersion allows you to study together and add comments and questions in the group reading plan. Then, as you complete your reading plan, take turns selecting different reading plans.

sunday stroll

For this Sunday Stroll, I want you and your spouse to do just that. Go out for on a long walk. No phone, children, or work. Take the time to enjoy one another's company while taking in your surroundings.

While walking, talk about your thoughts and experiences from the previous section and throughout this book. Assess where you and your spouse are concerning the many topics discussed as well.

Toward the end of your walk (or after), discuss what it means for you to walk together for a lifetime.

conclusion

Two are better than one because they have a more satisfying return for their labor; for if either of them falls, the one will lift up his companion. But woe to him who is alone when he falls and does not have another to lift him up. Again, if two lie down together, then they keep warm; but how can one be warm alone? And though one can overpower him who is alone, two can resist him. A cord of three strands is not quickly broken.
Ecclesiastes 4:9-12 AMP

Through this short study guide, I pray you and your spouse are hopeful about walking together in marriage. Though there might be many other discussions and exercises to accomplish along the way, I pray this guide was a catalyst for encouraging you to reach your destination in Christ together.

Marriage can be a beautiful reflection of Jesus' love for the church. I pray He provides you with the wisdom, mercy, grace, and peace to navigate through the rocky paths of your relationship toward paths that are lighted by Him (Psalm 119:105). May the love you share propel your marriage further and encourage many others to pursue the same.

I want to thank you again for using this study guide to help you and your spouse. I consider it an honor for God to use such a resource for His glory. May the Lord bless you and keep you.

endnotes

1 "4 Types of Communication Styles." Alvernia University. Web. March 27, 2018. https://online.alvernia.edu/articles/4-types-communication-styles/.

2 "Variables in the Study of Conflict." Communication Institute for Online Scholarship. http://www.cios.org/encyclopedia/conflict/Dvariables9_style.htm.

(com)mission
PUBLISHING

www.commissionpubs.com
info@commissionpubs.com

Made in the USA
Columbia, SC
25 February 2021